Collins
INTERNATIONAL

Science Foundation

Activity Book B

Published by Collins
An imprint of HarperCollins*Publishers*
The News Building, 1 London Bridge Street,
London, SE1 9GF, UK

HarperCollins*Publishers*
Macken House, 39/40 Mayor Street Upper,
Dublin 1, DO1 C9W8, Ireland

Browse the complete Collins catalogue at
www.collins.co.uk

British Library Cataloguing-in-Publication Data
A catalogue record for this publication is available from the British Library.

Author: Fiona Macgregor
Publisher: Elaine Higgleton
Product manager: Letitia Luff
Commissioning editor: Rachel Houghton
Edited by: Eleanor Barber
Editorial management: Oriel Square
Cover designer: Kevin Robbins
Cover illustrations: Jouve India Pvt Ltd.
Internal illustrations: Jouve India Pvt. Ltd.;
p 11tl, p 17, p19, p20–21 Tasneem Amiruddin
Typesetter: Jouve India Pvt. Ltd.
Production controller: Lyndsey Rogers
Printed and Bound in the UK using 100% Renewable
Electricity at Martins the Printers

Acknowledgements

With thanks to all the kindergarten staff and their schools around the world who have helped with the development of this course, by sharing insights and commenting on and testing sample materials:

Calcutta International School: Sharmila Majumdar, Mrs Pratima Nayar, Preeti Roychoudhury, Tinku Yadav, Lakshmi Khanna, Mousumi Guha, Radhika Dhanuka, Archana Tiwari, Urmita Das; Gateway College (Sri Lanka): Kousala Benedict; Hawar International School: Kareen Barakat, Shahla Mohammed, Jennah Hussain; Manthan International School: Shalini Reddy; Monterey Pre-Primary: Adina Oram; Prometheus School: Aneesha Sahni, Deepa Nanda; Pragyanam School: Monika Sachdev; Rosary Sisters High School: Samar Sabat, Sireen Freij, Hiba Mousa; Solitaire Global School: Devi Nimmagadda; United Charter Schools (UCS): Tabassum Murtaza; Vietnam Australia International School: Holly Simpson

The publishers wish to thank the following for permission to reproduce photographs.

(t = top, c = centre, b = bottom, r = right, l = left)

p 22t Tommy Pavasut/Shutterstock, p 22c1 A Sharma/Shutterstock, p 22c2 schubbel/Shutterstock, p 22b djgis/Shutterstock

Extracts from Collins Big Cat readers reprinted by permission of HarperCollins *Publishers* Ltd

All © HarperCollins*Publishers*

MIX
Paper | Supporting
responsible forestry
FSC™ C007454

This book contains FSC™ certified paper and other controlled sources to ensure responsible forest management.

For more information visit:
www.harpercollins.co.uk/green

Match

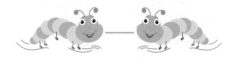

air

soil

sun

water

What do plants need?
Match the pictures to the words.   Date:

Draw

How did you look after your plant?
Draw a picture.

Date:

Circle

Circle the things a goat needs to stay
alive and be healthy.

Date:

Cut and stick

What my body needs

PCM 7. Cut out and stick the pictures which show the things you need to stay alive and be healthy.   Date:

5

Follow

Help the animals find their habitats.

Date:

Cut and stick

Water animals

PCM 9. Cut out and stick the pictures
of animals that live in water.   Date:

Draw

Draw the animal in its habitat.

Date:

Match

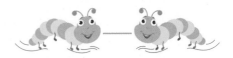

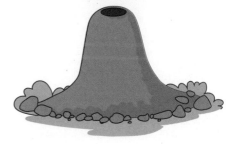

Help the animals find their habitats.

Date:

Tick and say

☐   rain

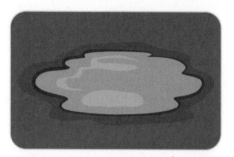
☐   puddle

☐   river

☐   sea

Where have you seen water? Tick and say.

Date:

Follow

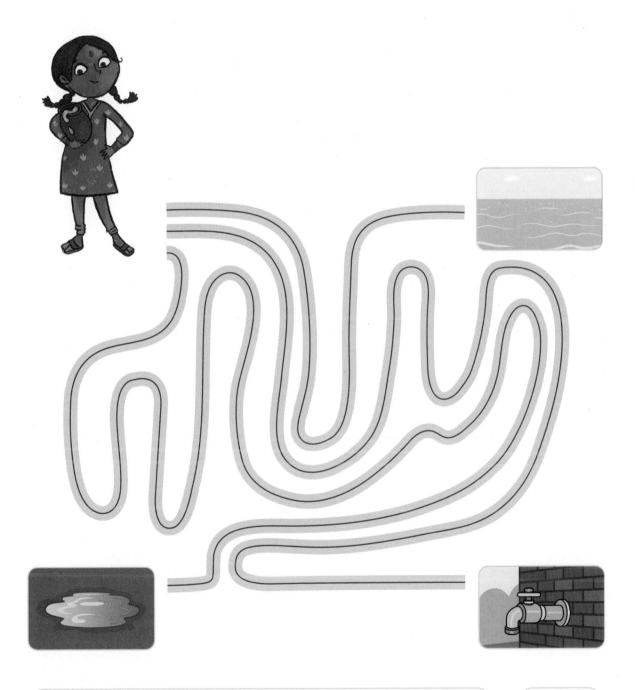

Help Ana get clean, fresh water.
Find the correct path.

Date:

11

Colour

☐ cups of water

Colour in one cup every time you drink some water today.
How many cups did you drink? Write the number.   Date:

Tick and say

☐ wash

☐ cook

☐ drink

☐ grow

Why do people and animals need water?
Tick and say.

Date:

Write

This is me.

Draw a picture of yourself as a baby.
Write your name.   Date:

Put in order

1	2
3	4

PCM 11. Cut out the pictures.
Stick them in the correct order.   Date:

Match

A sheep and its lambs.   A cat and its kittens.

A goat and its kid.   Two hens and
                          their chicks.

PCM 12. Cut out the pictures.
Stick them above the correct sentences.   Date:

Match

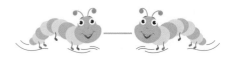

Help the baby animals find the adult animals.

Date:

Sort

Day

Night

PCM 14. Colour the boxes. Cut out the pictures.
Stick them in the correct box.   Date:

Draw and say

Draw a sun next to the picture if it is day.
Draw a moon if it is night.

Date:

Circle

Circle all the sources of light.

Date:

Draw

Draw a torch or a light bulb.

Date:

Match

The sun gives light.

Plants need sun.

A goat and its kid.

We drink water.

Match the sentences to the pictures.

Date:

Tick

☐ I can match.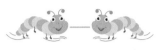

☐ I can draw.

☐ I can circle.

☐ I can cut and stick.

☐ I can follow.

☐ I can tick and say.

☐ I can colour.

☐ I can write.

☐ I can put in order.

☐ I can sort.

☐ I can draw and say.

Tick what you can do.

Date:

Assessment record

_____ has achieved these Science Foundation Phase Objectives:

Name things plants need to stay alive	1	2	3
Name things animals need to stay alive	1	2	3
Recognise that different animals make or find different homes	1	2	3
Know that some animals live on land and others live in water	1	2	3
Identify sources of water	1	2	3
Understand uses of water	1	2	3
Recognise that living things grow and change	1	2	3
Describe similarities and differences between adult animals and their young	1	2	3
Know the names of some young animals	1	2	3
Describe the concept of day and night	1	2	3
Recognise the repeating patterns of day and night	1	2	3
Identify light sources we use in the dark	1	2	3
Know that some of these sources depend on electricity	1	2	3

1: Partially achieved
2: Achieved
3: Exceeded

Signed by teacher:
Signed by parent: Date: